British Railway Pictorial

Railways of Devon and Cornwall

Anthony Burges

CONTENTS

ACKNOWLEDGEMENTS

This opportunity to relive good times past would not have been possible without the assistance of my old friend Gerald Siviour in supplementing my photographs with some of his own. Once again the technical expertise of Michael Bowie of Lux Photographic Services of Carleton Place, Ontario, has been an essential ingredient in bringing history to life.

Anthony W. Burges
Ottawa

This book is dedicated to my grandson Seamus Burges-Sims in the hope that he will uphold the family railway tradition.

First published 2008

ISBN 978 0 7110 3298 9

All rights reserved. No part of this book may be reproduced or transmitted in any form or by any means, electronic or mechanical, including photocopying, recording or by any information storage and retrieval system, without permission from the Publisher in writing.

© Anthony Burges 2008

Published by Ian Allan Publishing

an imprint of Ian Allan Publishing Ltd, Hersham, Surrey KT12 4RG
Printed in England by Ian Allan Printing Ltd

Code: 0805/B1

Visit the Ian Allan Publishing website at www.ianallanpublishing.com

All photographs are by the author unless otherwise credited.

Above: The North Devon & Cornwall Junction Light Railway was one of the shortest-lived (1925-80), least-known and most poorly promoted backwaters of the Southern Railway; a single coach usually sufficed for the vestigial passenger service. As the two advertised weekday return trips covering the entire length of the line were designated as mixed, there was always time enough for the traveller to admire the neat fieldstone stations at Petrockstow, Hatherleigh and Hole. Devon & Cornwall Farmers Ltd was a freight customer at Petrockstow, and in this 21 July 1955 view the less-than-demanding schedule provides ample opportunity for the time-honoured banter between train crew and station staff that epitomised the friendly ambiance of the all-too-short lost age of light railways.

Title page: Heathfield was the junction of the Teign Valley line and the Newton Abbot-Moretonhampstead branch. In June 1958 '14xx' 0-4-2T No 1466 makes a brief stop with an Exeter-Newton Abbot train. Occasional freight services lingered on until recently, while sporadic industrial development has done little to improve the scene. *G. R. Siviour*

PREFACE

It is strange now to recall the sense of excitement and anticipation that the prospect of a summer holiday in the West Country induced in those grey years following the end of the Second World War. For the author an awareness of liberation was exemplified by the thrill of boarding the 'Atlantic Coast Express', which was not notably fast throughout much of its run, en route to a series of family visits, or more accurately, farm escapes, to places such as Colston Cross near Axminster, Lyme Regis on the Dorset-Devon border, the Sterridge Valley near Berrynarbor in North Devon and Widemouth Bay near Bude in North Cornwall. The 'ACE' was the Southern Region's 'everywhere west flagship' and its mix of coaches carried a bewildering variety of destination boards in accordance with the philosophy of 'divide the train and rule the territory'. An immediate concern was to ensure that my bicycle was labelled and stowed in the correct brake-van of a train that shrank in size as it put more miles between itself and Waterloo. None of the destinations served by the 'ACE' can now be reached by through rail service from Waterloo. The list is surprisingly long, extending from Sidmouth, Exmouth via Budleigh Salterton, Ilfracombe and Torrington to Plymouth, Bude and Padstow in the far west. Such was the demand from holidaymakers at the peak of the season that the train was run in several sections on Saturdays in the early postwar period.

Once under way, one experienced a certain satisfaction, or perhaps smugness, on sweeping past passengers lining the platforms of suburban stations or the fleeting glimpse of a solitary traveller awaiting a stopping train at Sutton Bingham. An added thrill was the initial headlong rush to Salisbury at an average speed of 60 miles per hour. This was enhanced by the whiff of steam and the dusting of smoke and cinders that drifted in through the partially open window. The auditory experience was memorable, ranging from the initial shuddering attempts of the Bulleid 'air-smoothed' Pacific at the head of the train to gain adhesion to the somewhat mournful wailing sounds that emanated from the locomotive's whistle. After claiming their seat reservations with some difficulty and occasionally protracted dispute, passengers settled down amidst the brown uncut moquette upholstery in compartments adorned with faded sepia views of such scenic delights as Budleigh Salterton. For the author Salisbury represented the frontier between the known and unknown world and an opportunity to watch the locomotive take water.

On departing from there each subtle change in scenery heightened the sense of expectation, which grew still more with a tantalising glimpse of the somewhat 'foreign'-looking Somerset & Dorset as we hurtled through Templecombe. Ahead lay the prospects of exploring a world of railways seemingly frozen in time where branch lines curved away into unknown territory and steam traction reigned supreme. Doubtless the enthusiast ensconced in the down 'Cornish Riviera' was enjoying similar feelings after leaving Paddington, but this was the Southern, holidays beckoned and concerns revolved around hopes for fine weather, an adequate supply of film and the prospect of scrumptious cream teas.

With the peacetime relaxation of constraints on travel, the South West still seemed to be both remote and slightly exotic. A 'runabout' ticket was to be the key to unlocking this world of delights. In those days it was a passport to freedom and adventure. Having been reared in a part of England where 'canine' preferences tended towards 'Greyhounds' and 'Terriers', I nonetheless hoped for a glimpse of an elderly 'Bulldog' beyond Exeter. What was not obvious at the time was that I was witnessing the last hurrah of the railways as an essential component of the summer holidays before growing affluence, increasing car ownership and air travel transformed the travel horizons of the masses. In the decades that followed I made use of abundant opportunities to revisit old railway haunts in the West of England while visiting from the USA and Canada and to witness the continuing transformation of the railways as they adapted to far-reaching socio-economic changes within the UK.

Right: In order to counter the general impression that Devon was perpetually bathed in sunshine during the summer months, here is a rain-drenched scene at Exeter St Davids on 28 June 1953 in which last surviving 'Star' class 4-6-0 No 4056 *Princess Margaret* is about to depart for Paddington via Bristol with an enthusiasts' special.

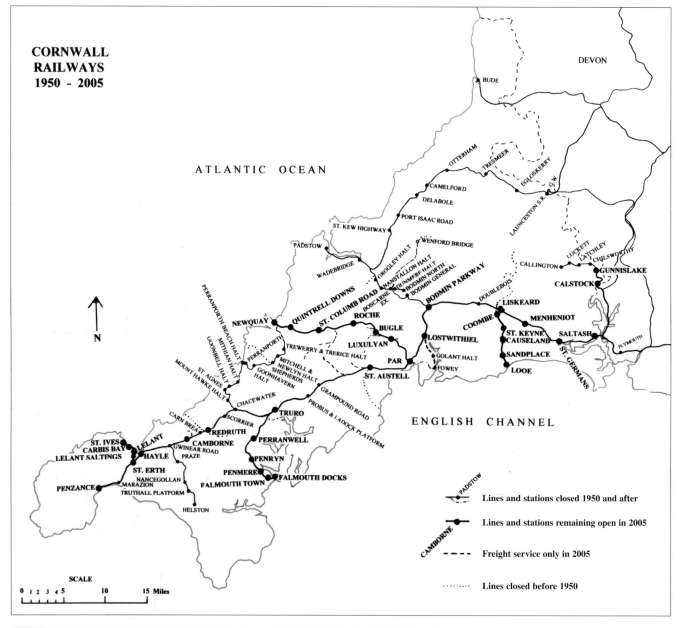

CORNWALL
RAILWAYS
1950 - 2005

ATLANTIC OCEAN

DEVON

N

ENGLISH CHANNEL

SCALE

0 1 2 3 4 5   10   15 Miles

PADSTOW ————— Lines and stations closed 1950 and after

CAMBORNE ——●—— Lines and stations remaining open in 2005

- - - - - Freight service only in 2005

· · · · · · · Lines closed before 1950

Closed stations litter the landscape of Devon and Cornwall. Happily their residential value is well understood and many are imaginatively nurtured by their new owners. One such example is Bridestowe, seen here in April 1971, where what was once part of a main line is now part of the Granite Way. In early days Bridestowe was formerly a junction for a spur serving peat workings on Dartmoor.

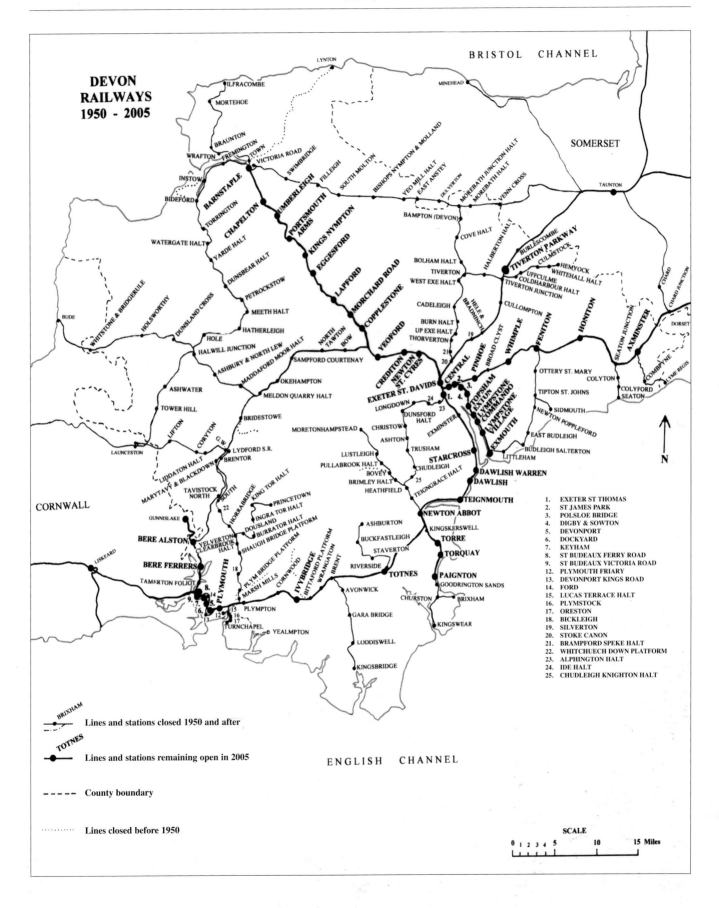

DEVON
RAILWAYS
1950 - 2005

BRISTOL CHANNEL

SOMERSET

CORNWALL

ENGLISH CHANNEL

1.   EXETER ST THOMAS
2.   ST JAMES PARK
3.   POLSLOE BRIDGE
4.   DIGBY & SOWTON
5.   DEVONPORT
6.   DOCKYARD
7.   KEYHAM
8.   ST BUDEAUX FERRY ROAD
9.   ST BUDEAUX VICTORIA ROAD
12. PLYMOUTH FRIARY
13. DEVONPORT KINGS ROAD
14. FORD
15. LUCAS TERRACE HALT
16. PLYMSTOCK
17. ORESTON
18. BICKLEIGH
19. SILVERTON
20. STOKE CANON
21. BRAMPFORD SPEKE HALT
22. WHITCHUECH DOWN PLATFORM
23. ALPHINGTON HALT
24. IDE HALT
25. CHUDLEIGH KNIGHTON HALT

BRIXHAM — Lines and stations closed 1950 and after

TOTNES ● Lines and stations remaining open in 2005

- - - - - County boundary

· · · · · · · · · Lines closed before 1950

SCALE
0 1 2 3 4 5   10   15 Miles

Above: Bulleid 'West Country' light Pacific No 34013 *Okehampton* with the Padstow portion of the 'Atlantic Coast Express' climbs the Kensey Valley west of Egloskerry on 15 July 1955. After leaving Halwill this far-flung remnant of the flagship express of the Southern ran non-stop to Launceston with calls thereafter at Tresmeer, Otterham, Camelford, Delabole, Port Isaac Road and Wadebridge, before finally reaching the Atlantic shore at what was then the small fishing port and resort of Padstow located some 260 miles and 6 hours and 21 minutes from Waterloo. Clearly the definition of 'express' 50 years ago had as much to do with the omission of station stops as high speed!

Left: Lustleigh, seen here on 9 July 1952, was one of those stations, renowned for its beautiful gardens, tended by an obviously devoted station staff and here occupying land originally acquired for the provision of a passing loop that was never built. The village was, and remains, a quintessential Devon cluster of thatched and half-timbered cottages. It would have been difficult to surpass Lustleigh as an ideal location for a camping coach holiday. This idyllic spot also impressed the writer for its luggage label rack brimming with a treasure trove of South Devon Railway relics. It was sad to see the wilderness that overtook the station site after abandonment.

INTRODUCTION

The railway scene in the south-western counties of Devon and Cornwall underwent even more profound changes during the period from 1950 to the present than much of Southern England. Apart from the demise of steam traction, which was of course nationwide, the railway map was radically redrawn. Paradoxically, there appeared to be an inverse relationship between demographic trends and the evolution of the rail network. The population of Devon grew by approximately 37% over this period while that of Cornwall expanded at an even greater rate of 47%. Today, the combined population of the two counties has reached about 1.6 million compared to 1.14 million in 1951. On the other hand, this same period was one of massive retrenchment for the railways, with route mileage declining from 766 to 306 miles, a reduction of 60% (see Table 1). Concurrently the total number of stations open to regular passenger traffic, excluding those ultimately transferred to preserved heritage/tourist railways and tramways, declined from 263 to 83, of which only 27 remain staffed in 2005, representing an even greater reduction of 68.5% (see the maps on pages 4-5 and Table 2). However, these changes are not necessarily indicative of the domesday scenario they suggest and, in common with national trends, the surviving main-line components of the network are now being exploited on an increasingly intensive basis. Notwithstanding that caveat, the 55-year period brought evidence of an overly zealous approach to rationalisation, which in all fairness could not be expected to anticipate the forthcoming transformation of the lifestyles and economy of Britain.

Nonetheless, the scars inflicted on the rail network were severe and remain to this day. Thus the prevailing wisdom regarding the future role of the railways resulted in the imposition of severe constrictions on the capacity of the former SR main line from Salisbury to Exeter and on sections of the former GWR main line in Cornwall as double track was reduced to single track and signalling was simplified. Concurrently the main lines were refocused to emphasise their inter-city role and most of their intermediate country stations were eliminated. Extensive branch-line abandonments reflected the questionable philosophy that the logic of bus substitution would be embraced by a grateful public. In practice potential travellers were steadily opting for non-rail alternatives such as the private car or direct long-distance coach service. This failure, on the part of policy-makers, to take convenience factors into consideration created a situation in which it appeared, metaphorically speaking, that the baby was being thrown out with the bathwater. In the last 20 years there have been a few tentative signs of a reversal in this minimalist approach, and the construction of new stations at Tiverton Parkway, Lelant Saltings, Digby & Sowton, Ivybridge and Lympstone Commando, in addition to the reopening of closed stations at Feniton (formerly Sidmouth Junction) and Pinhoe, hinted at the beginnings of a slow reversal in policy. Furthermore there dawned an emerging awareness of the fragility of the remaining attenuated rail network in the context of climate change, escalating energy costs and an increasingly overburdened highway system.

But in 1950, before the axe fell, much of the totally steam-operated rail network in the two counties was, from the enthusiast's point of view, undeniably picturesque, but represented an accountant's nightmare dependent on ever-growing government subsidies. It was a nostalgic experience to enjoy vintage steam traction and rolling stock, although it was increasingly obvious that the railways were not efficiently responding to the needs of passengers and freight shippers. This was attested to by empty trains, short seasonal peaks in travel demand, increasing diversion of goods to road haulage, deserted country stations admired more for their floral displays than their relevance to passenger needs, and bus services, which although largely publicly owned, were expanding in direct competition with British Railways. Devon and Cornwall were, in more ways than one, stony ground on which to develop and maintain a complex rail network.

The physical barriers imposed by upland wilderness areas such as Dartmoor and Bodmin Moor historically impeded railway construction and resulted in circuitous routes while presenting less formidable obstacles for upgraded trunk highways in later years. Another unfortunate inheritance of the railways was that their prime objectives, such as the resort communities situated on rugged indented coastlines, were often difficult to reach because of the challenging topography. Thus stations were sometimes inconveniently sited, as at Ilfracombe and Brixham, and links to main lines could involve slow circuitous journeys characterised by heavy gradients and curvature that made them costly to operate, as on the North Cornwall line, and therefore decreasingly competitive in terms of journey time as car ownership increased and highways were improved.

The population distribution and other demographic characteristics of the region were not always ideal for rail transport. Apart from significant concentrations of population at Plymouth, Exeter, Torbay and, to a lesser extent, the Cornish county town of Truro, rail commuting potential was historically limited to a few local services often serving halts that were closed prior to 1950. More recently growth in the population of major urban centres is contributing to increasing traffic gridlock and has refocused the interest of planners in rail commuting. With a greater proportion of population in the over-65 age group than in much of southern England, the retirees, who are drawn to the South West by its climatic and scenic advantages, tend to travel less frequently than the working population. Further factors that contrast to the situation in the Home Counties closer to London are that communities in Devon and Cornwall are characterised by greater ranges in relative prosperity and poverty. Low population growth and density have continued to typify the northern areas of Devon and Cornwall where the population levels of some towns and villages have tended to remain stagnant or to decline.

THE WEST HAS CHANGED

With the notable exceptions of tourism and the service sector, the economic base of the region has evolved in ways that are decreasingly dependent on rail transport. Apart from the mining industry in Cornwall, the area was only marginally affected by the Industrial Revolution. Agriculture, mining and fishing activities are now less significant in relative terms than in the past. In the farm sector

TABLE 1
LINE CLOSURES, 1950-2005

A	Closed to all traffic and line abandoned
P	Closed to passengers
F	Closed to freight

Year	From	To	Type
1951	Plymouth Friary	Turnchapel	P
1956	Yelverton	Princetown	A[1]
1957	Topsham	Topsham Quay	F
1958	Totnes	Ashburton	P
	Exeter St Thomas	Heathfield	P
	Plymouth Friary	Plymouth North Road	P
1959	Newton Abbot	Moretonhampstead	P
1960	Plymstock	Yealmpton	F
1961	Plymouth Friary	Turnchapel	F
	Trusham	Christow	F
1962	Marsh Mills	Launceston[2]	A[1]
	Totnes	Ashburton[3]	F
1963	Brent	Kingsbridge	A
	Churston	Brixham	A
	Tiverton Junction	Hemyock	P
	Morebath Junction Halt	Exeter St Davids	A
	Looe	Looe Buller Quay	F
1964	Tiverton Junction	Tiverton	P
	Seaton Junction	Seaton	A[4]
	Bovey	Moretonhampstead	F
	Plymouth North Road	St Budeaux via Ford[5]	A
	Bugle	Wheal Rose	F

Year	From	To	Type
1965	Par	Fowey	F
	Halwill Junction	Meeth	A
	Meeth	Torrington	P
	Barnstaple Junction	Torrington	P
	Lostwithiel	Fowey	P
	Chudleigh	Trusham	F
	Par	Par Harbour	F
	Axminster	Lyme Regis	A
1966	Gwinear Road	Helston	A
	Chacewater	Newquay	A[6]
	Halwill Junction	Bude	A[1,7]
	Meldon Junction	Wadebridge	A[8]
	Gunnislake	Callington	A
	Norton Fitzwarren	Barnstaple Junction	A
1967	Dunmere Junction	Bodmin North	A[1]
	Bodmin Road	Padstow	P
	Heathfield	Chudleigh	F
	Sidmouth Junction	Exmouth	A
	Tipton St Johns	Sidmouth	A
1968	Meldon Quarry	Bere Alston	A[1]
1970	Barnstaple Junction	Ilfracombe	A[1]
	Devonport Kings Road	Stonehouse Pool	F
1972	Coleford Junction	Okehampton[9]	P
	Paignton	Kingswear[10]	A
1975	Tiverton Junction	Hemyock	F
1978	Bodmin Road	Wadebridge[11]	F[1,12]
1982	Barnstaple Junction	Torrington	F[1]
	Torrington	Meeth	F[1]

Notes

[1] All or part converted to trail after abandonment
[2] Section between Marsh Mills and Plym Bridge being restored by Plym Valley Railway
[3] Subsequently reopened by Dart Valley Railway (now South Devon Railway) between Totnes (Littlehempston) and Buckfastleigh
[4] Section of line subsequently reopened as narrow gauge Seaton Tramway
[5] Freight service continued from Devonport Junction to Devonport Kings Road until 1971
[6] Section between Wheal Rose and Newlyn Halt later reopened as narrow gauge Lappa Valley Railway
[7] Bude Quay branch closed to freight 1960
[8] Section between Launceston and New Mills later reopened as narrow gauge Launceston Steam Railway

[9] Reopened later for seasonal weekend service with freight continuing to Meldon Quarry. Also, Dartmoor Railway later commenced operations from Sampford Courtenay to Meldon.
[10] Transferred as seasonal tourist operation to Dart Valley Railway (now Paignton & Dartmouth Steam Railway). Closure also applied to Dartmouth, which was connected to Kingswear by ferry only.
[11] Reopened later as Bodmin & Wenford Railway from Bodmin Road (Parkway) to Bodmin General and Boscarne Junction
[12] Bodmin Road-Dunmere Junction-Wenford Bridge retained for china clay traffic until 1983

For further details of intermediate stations on closed sections see the maps on pages 4-5.

---

livestock production, which was once an important business for the railways, was long ago ceded to road transport. Similarly, large-scale milk traffic from locations throughout the region such as Hemyock, Seaton Junction, Totnes, Lapford, Crediton, Torrington, Lifton, Lostwithiel, Camborne and St Erth, which was shipped in multiple tank wagon lots to markets as far away as London, has been lost. Since 1950 there has also been consolidation in the milk and milk products industry, which now relies exclusively on road transport.

Cut flowers from the Scilly Isles were shipped to market by rail from Penzance, while early vegetables and flowers were loaded at stations such as Helston, Gwinear Road, St Erth, Marazion and Penzance. Foreign competition has adversely affected this business and what remains is handled by road and air transport. Supply and resource management problems have resulted in a decline in the Cornish fishery at ports such as Newlyn. The tin-mining industry around Redruth and Camborne was already declining during the rail

construction era and is now defunct. The china clay industry, served by a network of dedicated rail lines near St Austell and the port of Fowey is slowly declining due to global competition, while outliers of production on the fringes of Dartmoor include locations such as the clay works at Lee Moor, which at one time supported a horse-drawn tramway connecting it to Plymouth, and has recently ceased operation.

The extensive naval dockyards and associated shore establishments of the

TABLE 2
STATION CLOSURES ON LINES THAT REMAINED OPEN FOR PASSENGER TRAFFIC IN 2005

Year	Station	Year	Station	Year	Station
1957	Probus & Ladock Platform	1964	Gwinear Road	1964	Exminster
1959	Bittaford Platform		Marazion		Brent
	Cornwood		Scorrier		Kingskerswell
	Plympton		Doublebois		Seaton Junction
1960	Ivybridge[1]		Burlescombe	1966	Pinhoe[3]
1962	Tamerton Foliot		Sampford Peverell[2]	1967	Sidmouth Junction[4]
1963	Wrangaton		Cullompton	1972	Bow
1964	Carn Brea		Hele & Bradninch		North Tawton
	Chacewater		Silverton	1986	Tiverton Junction[5]
	Grampound Road		Stoke Canon		

Notes
[1] Replaced by new station at different location
[2] Site of new Tiverton Parkway, 1986
[3] Reopened 1983
[4] Reopened as Feniton, 1971
[5] Replaced by Tiverton Parkway at different location, 1986

For details of closed stations on open lines see the maps on pages 4-5.

Royal Navy at Plymouth and Devonport are a shadow of their former glory and other military facilities such as air bases in Cornwall and army training zones on Dartmoor have been reduced in scale. Furthermore the growth of manufacturing activity has not been as significant as that of the service sector, in which the decentralisation of government departments and agencies together with other business activities has been beneficial for Exeter and Plymouth. Here the impacts have been reflected in inter-city and commuter passenger rail demand. The situation for freight traffic as far as the rail network is concerned consists of little more than the short haul of china clay from origin points in the Goonbarrow area to the port of Fowey, and trainload movements of cement from a plant at Moorswater on the Looe branch.

Essentially the two counties are no longer the fertile ground for railways that they were during the 19th and first half of the 20th century. Then the railways enjoyed a virtual monopoly of the tourist traffic. Tourist-oriented communities such as Ilfracombe, Bideford, Bude, Port Isaac, Wadebridge, Padstow, Perranporth, Fowey, Kingsbridge, Brixham, Kingswear/Dartmouth, Sidmouth, Seaton and, across the Dorset border, Lyme Regis, are no longer served by the national rail network, while Newquay remains connected by a slender thread. Although tourism remains a keystone of the economy, high levels of car ownership in the UK have resulted in an increasing use of motorway and trunk highway linkages provided by the M5, A30, A38, A361 and the Tamar road bridge. Collectively, improvements in road connections have been a significant factor in diminishing the perceived remoteness of the region and door-to-door travel times can often be competitive with rail. Low-cost air travel has resulted in a transformation of both business and leisure travel in Europe and the UK, and busy international airports now flourish at Exeter and Plymouth, while the regional airport at Newquay offers expanding domestic air linkages. Railways no longer play a role in connecting to cross-Channel ferries while regular ocean liner services have ceased to call at Plymouth, which now caters increasingly to cruise ships. These developments have rendered the GWR boat trains to Plymouth Millbay and those operated by the LSWR to Stonehouse Pool but a distant memory.

Today a wide swath of the South West comprising most of North Devon and much of North Cornwall is devoid of railways and presents a blank on the map comparable to that of the border counties of Scotland and Northern Ireland. Unquestionably the railway now plays a greatly modified role in Devon and Cornwall but one that is increasingly valued in an age where energy costs and environmental concerns are of increasing importance.

OBJECTIVES

Thus the aims of this book are to temper nostalgia with realism. It is hoped that a blend of fond reminiscences and a review of the changes that have occurred may establish a context within which the reader can take a balanced approach to the contemporary rail network. Others have laboured long and diligently in recording the history of the railways and any bibliography would be quite voluminous. Instead the reader is encouraged to consult the copious library, internet and video resources that are available. This modest summary is necessarily very selective and subject to rigorous space limitations, and the author freely admits to certain biases that may emerge in both the text and still more in the photo captions. Old railway memories tend, like a fine wine, to take on a changed character with age, but it is hoped that something of the flavour and bouquet of a past era lingers here.

A FADING PRESENCE

As noted, topographical impediments, demographic characteristics, changes in the regional economy and intense modal competition have combined to create a more limited yet focused role for the railways. It is reasonable to assert that as early as 1950 many branch lines and country stations were suffering heavy losses that could not be sustained indefinitely. It was therefore no great surprise that the Beeching report in 1963 concluded that draconian measures were justified. Its recommendation that passenger services be withdrawn from 22 sections of line in Devon and Cornwall was subsequently implemented with only the Liskeard-Looe, St Erth-St Ives and Exeter Central-Exmouth lines escaping the axe. A partial survivor was the Plymouth-Gunnislake portion of the Callington branch service. The surgery also included seven mostly main-line sections where small intermediate country stations were identified as targets. Thus many of these disappeared. The Salisbury-Exeter route was downgraded and rail facilities in Cornwall as envisioned by Beeching were to be cut back, leaving only three routes comprising the main line to Penzance plus the branches to Newquay and Falmouth. Elsewhere in this category only the Exeter-Barnstaple Junction portion of the old main line to Ilfracombe in Devon survived. Study of the maps on pages 4-5 illustrates in graphic terms the amount of rationalisation that actually occurred.

In addition, there were a further seven lines that were either under consideration for closure or in process of being closed during the Beeching period. Of these all but the Culm Valley line from Tiverton Junction to Hemyock were rapidly abandoned. Full implementation of the Beeching proposals would have reduced the number of stations remaining open in Devon and Cornwall from the current total of 83 to 44. This, together with all of the line abandonments, would have resulted in an even more drastic implosion of the network accompanied by the replacement of steam traction and the loss of freight traffic. It can be argued that the analysis underpinning this plan failed to take into

account the fact that severing the limbs from the tree can weaken the health of the trunk. Nonetheless Devon and Cornwall have had to live with the consequences that have already been referred to. Thus, with the exception of some residual but declining china clay movements and bulk cement traffic, Plymouth is now the western freight railhead, and the long-term future of some branch-line services is uncertain as governments periodically wrestle with funding priorities for transport infrastructure.

As the rail network imploded and steam traction was replaced by diesel, a familiar feature, the locomotive shed, was an obvious victim. There were no fewer than 26 sheds in Devon and Cornwall in 1950. The larger depots were generally located at major junctions, while virtually every branch line possessed a shed at the terminus. On the lines of the former Southern Railway the first shed to close was Torrington in 1959. It was followed in the succeeding years by Launceston, Plymouth Friary, Exmouth, Seaton, Lyme Regis (located just across the border in Dorset), Callington, Bude, Barnstaple

Junction, Ilfracombe, Wadebridge and Okehampton, and finally Exmouth Junction in 1967. On the lines of the former GWR there were major locomotive depots at Plymouth Laira, Newton Abbot (where there were also workshops), Exeter, St Blazey, Truro and Penzance, with smaller sub-sheds at Bodmin, Princetown, Moretonhampstead, Ashburton, Kingsbridge, St Ives, Helston, Launceston, Tiverton Junction and Moorswater. Only a vastly changed Laira and St Blazey remain to serve the transformed railway network of today.

After teetering on the edge of the Beeching abyss the railways completed the elimination of steam power on the Western Region by uniquely, but in true Swindon tradition, opting for diesel-hydraulic rather than diesel-electric traction for its replacement locomotive fleet. Decisions were made to designate the former GWR main line as the principal route to the West. This consigned the Southern route west of Salisbury to a secondary status and had the effect of dooming most of the former Southern network beyond Exeter to eventual oblivion. Thus the 'withered arm',

Left: Barnstaple Junction shed was one of the 26 to be found in Devon in 1950. On 21 July 1955 'E1R' 0-6-2T No 32696 is on shed, one of a class that performed mostly on the North Devon & Cornwall Junction mixed service between Torrington and Halwill and on ball clay workings to Fremington Quay. Originally seven members of the class were allocated to Barnstaple, of which three were normally based at Torrington.

Right: Wadebridge was the most westerly shed on the Southern, and was the home of the three surviving '0298' class 2-4-0T Beattie well tanks used for working the Wenford Bridge branch, which was renowned for its curvature, gradients, weight restrictions and fine scenery. No 30587 is being coaled before working a load of china clay empties up the legendary branch on the fringes of Bodmin Moor.

as the Southern routes beyond Exeter were collectively known, either atrophied and died or survived in a truncated form. Here then was another debating issue (the 'What if...? question), which can only be of academic interest now.

A LAST BACKWARD LOOK

Today it is easy to overlook just how difficult it could often be to visit many of the remoter branch lines in the era before near universal car ownership. A lot of planning and physical exertion could be involved. For example, a visit to Hemyock from Lyme Regis involved a circuitous but interesting journey by train with changes at Axminster, Exeter St Davids and Tiverton Junction. On arrival at Hemyock the writer was then confronted with a fairly brisk hike across the hills to make an essential connection with a Saturdays-only market-day bus, which was nearly missed as it turned round in a farmyard at Dunkeswell. At Honiton it was back by train to Axminster before enjoying the familiar throaty sound of the Adams Radial as it struggled to lift the solitary coach over the hills to Lyme Regis.

Another memorable trip was my one and only visit to the Wenford Bridge branch. This entailed an early morning departure from Widemouth Bay by bicycle to connect with a Padstow train at Otterham. After loading the bike into the van I had a choice of seats in the comfortable Bulleid coaches as there were only three other passengers on the train. On arrival at Wadebridge the station was fairly bustling with activity, and after getting the paperwork out of the way at the station master's office, I had no difficulty in locating the Beattie well tank in the yard at the head of its trainload of empty china clay wagons for Wenford. There was plenty of room in the rough-riding non-fitted brake-van for the bike and there followed a couple of hours of bliss as we took water in the magic Pencarrow Wood and carefully negotiated ungated level crossings. Then it was a series of back-breaking hills on deserted country lanes with a brief stop to see the down 'ACE' at Delabole, and arrival back at the farm tired but happy.

The Yelverton-Princetown branch was unlike any other line in the West of England. The steep gradients and winding route as the line climbed to the highest station of the former Great Western Railway at Princetown were more reminiscent of the highlands of Scotland than the lush countryside that typifies much of Devon. This was certainly a line on which the fireman worked hard in one direction and relaxed on the return run. It possessed some of the most isolated halts in the county. With no road access, the intrepid traveller was unlikely to encounter any living creature except the Dartmoor ponies on alighting at Ingra Tor Halt. It was on the Princetown train that one would occasionally encounter two grim-faced men sitting closely together. Averting one's eyes from the handcuffs, one could be sure that one of them was not making the journey to enjoy the scenery. The branch left the world of living railways on a day when the moor was appropriately shrouded in swirling mist in which visiting enthusiasts shivered as they paid their last respects.

Although one of the last light railways to be built in Britain, the Halwill-Torrington line was also one of the most obscure. To travel in its empty one-coach train was to reach the nearest approach to the back of beyond that could be found. It maintained a decidedly reticent presence at both Halwill and Torrington, and its intermediate stations and halts, of which Hole was particularly memorable, seemed to be in the middle of nowhere. Even the principal intermediate station at Hatherleigh was a long walk from the sleepy town. I was privileged to savour its remoteness and evolving range of motive power beginning with elderly 'E1R' tanks followed by their BR Standard replacements and finally the incongruous and underpowered North British diesel-hydraulics. A walk or cycle ride is recommended along the trail that now follows much of its route. It is doubtful whether this timeless countryside has changed much since the days when the leisurely mixed train passed this way.

My travel records evoke a host of such memories peppered by recollections of the friendly welcome that was always extended by train crews and station staff. It is sad to reflect that none of these journeys have been possible for many years, but it was a privilege to have experienced such delights.

A NEW DAWN

Putting nostalgia aside, it is appropriate to briefly consider the contemporary role of railways in Devon and Cornwall. It is heartening to see that there is a growing public concern for environmental and quality-of-life issues. This has resonated at the political level so that the essential contribution of the railways is increasingly recognised. In Devon and Cornwall this is exemplified by the upgrading of main lines, an increasing focus on rail

Right: A few hardy railway enthusiasts shiver in the swirling mist at King Tor Halt as '45xx' 2-6-2T No 4568 arrives with a crowded train for Yelverton on the last day of operation, 3 March 1956.

commuting, the blossoming of community rail partnerships, a recognition of a role for rail in mitigating the traffic congestion problems threatening some tourist destinations, an acknowledgement of the well-established contribution of heritage/tourist railways to the regional economy, and awareness of the recreation value of abandoned railway rights of way as popular trails for hikers and cyclists.

1 Capacity constraints on the two main lines linking Penzance to London (Paddington) and Exeter to London (Waterloo) are receiving more attention. Single-line bottlenecks on the former GWR main line from Plymouth to Penzance have been eased with selective track improvements, while the former SR route between Salisbury and Exeter may be on the threshold of regaining prominence as the restoration of double-track sections, lifted as part of the Beeching inheritance, moves closer to reality. The shabby wreck that was Plymouth North Road station in the 1950s was replaced by a structure more worthy of the city. Tiverton Parkway station, opened on the site of the former Sampford Peverell station in 1986, represented a praiseworthy attempt to combine the ease of motorway access and convenience of adequate parking facilities with the public transport requirements of the growing town of Tiverton and an array of surrounding villages, many of which had been deprived of rail service in the years after 1950. Major population centres such as Penzance, Truro, Plymouth, Newton Abbot, Torbay and Exeter are now served by relatively fast and well-patronised trains, and, by 1950 standards, were, in 2005, linked to an unprecedented range of destinations throughout Britain by Virgin Cross Country services.

2 Rail commuting to Exeter from stations on the Exmouth branch is flourishing and a new suburban station was opened at Digby & Sowton in 1986, replacing the long-lost Clyst St Mary & Digby Halt. A growing number of commuters are now travelling to Exeter from Axminster, Honiton, Feniton, Whimple and Pinhoe, and the provision of an augmented service on this section is a possibility. Both Feniton and Pinhoe were reopened in response to local pressure. Commuting to Plymouth has been largely confined to services linking the city with St Germans, Liskeard and stations on the Gunnislake branch. A new station at Ivybridge has not generated the anticipated traffic. Convenience factors attributable to

the existence of trunk-road links, rail-service levels and the Tamar road bridge may also inhibit commuter growth. Special needs have been met with the opening of a private station at Lympstone Commando on the Exmouth branch.

3 The advent of community rail partnerships is involving the local population more closely in the role of the St Ives, Falmouth, Newquay, Looe, Gunnislake and Barnstaple lines, although responsibility for infrastructure investment, allocation of rolling stock and service frequencies resides with government departments, regulatory agencies, train-operating companies and Network Rail. There remain unresolved issues relating to an emphasis on the status quo by minimising costs as opposed to more pro-active approaches to planning, co-ordination, financing, management and control.

4 The opening of Lelant Saltings station on the St Ives branch in 1978 was a pioneer approach to addressing the seasonal traffic congestion that was threatening the popular coastal resort of St Ives with gridlock. Park-and-ride facilities of this type may be appropriate in other resort areas such as Looe. Devon County Council has similarly recognised the benefits to be derived from encouraging the diversion of visitors to rail when highways are particularly busy by subsidising a special seasonal Sunday service linking Exeter and Okehampton.

5 The railway preservation movement continues to be very successful in the two counties with passenger services operated by heritage/tourist railways on a profit or non-profit basis by the Paignton & Dartmouth Steam Railway (Paignton to Kingswear), South Devon Railway (Totnes [Littlehempston] to Buckfastleigh), Dartmoor Railway (Okehampton to Meldon and Sampford Courtenay), Bodmin & Wenford Railway (Bodmin General to Bodmin Parkway and Boscarne Junction), and the electrified narrow-gauge Seaton Tramway from Seaton to Colyton. In addition there are steam narrow-gauge lines such as the Launceston Steam Railway, which utilises several miles of the former LSWR North Cornwall line west from Launceston in the direction of Egloskerry, and the Lappa Valley Steam Railway, which follows a section of the former Chacewater-Newquay line at Wheal Rose. Reactivation of other

abandoned lines currently in progress includes the Plym Valley Railway (Marsh Mills to Clearbrook) and a section of the famous Lynton & Barnstaple narrow-gauge line at Woody Bay. Other attractions for visitors and enthusiasts include the Devon Railway Centre at Bickleigh and the Bicton Woodland Railway at East Budleigh.

6 There has been quite a widespread conversion of former railway rights of way for recreational purposes. Among the more notable routes are those connecting Meldon to Lydford (the Granite Way), Clearbrook to Marsh Mills (Plym Valley Cycle Trail), Braunton to Meeth (the Tarka Trail), Bodmin North to Padstow (the Camel Trail), and Princetown to Burrator (the Railway Trail). Additional trails are likely to be created in future years.

A CAUTIONARY NOTE

West of Exeter the former GWR main line from London to Penzance is now the only remaining rail link to Plymouth and the West. An exposed section of this route, which hugs the picturesque coastline in the vicinity of Dawlish, is increasingly vulnerable to coastal erosion. Services have been interrupted several times as a result of storms in which diesel locomotives and multiple-units have been immobilised due to salt water ingestion.

Climate change studies clearly indicate that sea levels are rising and weather conditions are becoming more unstable. The threat to the region's main rail line is very real. Whereas potential or actual alternate routes around the danger zone existed at one time, this is no longer the case. The Teign Valley line of the former GWR from Exeter to Heathfield and Newton Abbot at one time offered a limited-capacity alternative route but this has now been abandoned and is blocked by trunk road construction near Chudleigh. The former Southern Railway main line from Exeter to Plymouth now exists only between Cowley Bridge Junction, Exeter, and Meldon Quarry, west of Okehampton. Even if this route was available in its entirety, its junctions at Exeter and Plymouth face the wrong direction for through trains and severe operating problems would result. There is an urgent need to initiate contingency planning for an inevitably costly rail by-pass route in the Dawlish area as reinforcement of the sea wall is not likely to provide adequate protection on an ongoing basis.

1. EAST DEVON

CHARD BRANCH

Right: Beginning our journey across the border in Somerset, the seldom-visited line from Chard Junction to Taunton was of special interest in that the town of Chard formerly possessed two stations. In July 1952 '4575' 2-6-2T No 5501 passes the remains of the former LSWR station with a train for Chard Junction on the SR main line.

Below: Time seemed to have stood still at the sadly neglected Chard Joint station, which bore the imprint of the Bristol & Exeter Railway and its broad gauge ancestry. No 5501 has arrived from Taunton and is about to complete its journey to Chard Junction.

LYME REGIS BRANCH

Left: Proof that there was 'life in an old dog yet'! On 28 June 1953 enthusiasts were treated to a memorable high-speed run in appalling weather from Salisbury behind 'Greyhound' No 30711, seen here at a very wet Axminster station. Major track and infrastructure changes were soon to occur here and the closure of the Lyme Regis branch was to mean the loss of what was arguably the most beautiful byway of the Southern.

Below: The Lyme Regis line could only be described as glorious. Not only was it the last redoubt of the magnificent Class 0415 Adams Radial 4-4-2Ts but also a branch that offered the traveller unsurpassed scenery with the delightful port of Lyme Regis at its terminus. No 30584 is rounding a sharp curve as it approaches Combpyne with its two-coach train in June 1956. *G. R. Siviour*

Right: The switchback nature of the line and an abundance of curvature made a journey on the branch both an auditory and a visual experience to remember. In June 1956 No 30584 is halfway between Axminster and Combpyne.
G. R. Siviour

Above: No 30584 returns bunker-first to Axminster making the usual stop at Combpyne and thereby demonstrating a further justification for camping coach holidays at this delightful place. *G. R. Siviour*

Left: In July 1964, with one year remaining before closure, diesel multiple-units (DMUs) were a poor substitute for the Radial tanks. Passengers alight at the mysteriously haphazard station at Combpyne. No longer does the camping coach occupy the overgrown siding.

Above: The unconventional layout at Combpyne, seen here on 28 June 1953, included a station house, combining living quarters with a ticket office, toilets and waiting room, offset from the platform. Originally the station had an island platform plus two loops and livestock loading facilities, which tended to gently fade away in the later years. A truncated portion of one of the loops housed the camping coach for those who wanted peace and quiet with reasonable access by rail. Such was the isolation of Combpyne that no provision was made for a substitute bus service after closure in 1965.

Below: Adhesion problems on slippery rails are encountered by the unusual combination of Radial No 30583 and 'Terrier' No 32662 as they struggle to lift an enthusiasts' special destined for Lyme Regis out of Combpyne on 26 August 1953.

Above: The most notable engineering feature on the light railway was the 600-foot-long viaduct that carried the line across the Cannington Valley between Combpyne and Lyme Regis. In July 1952 No 30583 is returning to Axminster and has reached the point where the structure attains its maximum elevation of 92 feet above the valley floor. Reinforcement necessitated by the structural instability of one arch disturbs the symmetry of the bridge, which still survives as a local concrete landmark.

Below: Beyond Combpyne No 30584 is working hard as it climbs away from the Cannington Valley viaduct with a Lyme Regis train in June 1956. *G. R. Siviour*

Above: As it approaches the Devon/Dorset border near Uplyme during June 1956, No 30584 is once again working harder than might be expected from a veteran that began life on London suburban services. *G. R. Siviour*

Right: No 30583 climbs through hilly country leaving Lyme Regis with a one-coach train for Axminster in July 1952.

Below: On 26 August 1953 Nos 30583 and 32662 coast downhill through Uplyme on the final mile to the terminus at Lyme Regis on a second run from Axminster as part of an RCTS 25th anniversary railtour.

Right: The Adams Radials were undoubtedly a beautiful design. In July 1952 No 30583 has just arrived with its single coach at the hilltop station overlooking Lyme Regis. Station staff are unloading a few parcels but passengers are depressingly absent. Freight traffic lasted until the end and consisted largely of the inevitable household coal.

Below: On the same day No 30583 runs around its one-coach train at Lyme Regis. Note on the right the corridor coach that provided a through connection from Waterloo and was detached from a main-line train at Axminster.

Below: Bathed in summer sunshine No 30584 runs around its train at Lyme Regis in June 1956. Note the single-engine loco shed, and the ground frame at the end of the platform. The rural surroundings indicate the impossibility of extending the line to a more central site closer to the centre of the town, which covered the slopes between station and sea. *G. R. Siviour*

SEATON BRANCH

Left: Seaton Junction, seen here in July 1964, was an archetypal, if slightly modernised, country junction set amidst beautiful rolling countryside on the former LSWR main line between Axminster and Honiton. Apart from being the interchange for the short Seaton branch, it was also a passing place on the main line and the location of a dairy, now closed, which made heavy use of rail transport. A recent visit was a *déjà vu* experience as the fabric of the station buildings and platforms had remained undisturbed although the track layout is much reduced. In addition, today's DMUs that work the attenuated former main line from Waterloo ignore Seaton Junction and their passengers are unaware of this once important station.

Above: A first-generation DMU en route to Seaton Junction blends in well with the patchwork quilt of fields north of Colyton in July 1964. The glowering sky is, however, suggestive of the imminent closure of the Seaton branch.

Right: Colyton, photographed on 3 August 1958, was the principal intermediate station on the short but busy branch line linking Seaton Junction to the coastal resort of Seaton. Judging by the number of vans in the yard the volume of goods traffic handled there was quite healthy. Note the somewhat unusual provision of a water tower for the use of down trains despite the existence of facilities at Seaton. Today the traveller standing on the same spot might scan the horizon for a tram rather than a train.

Right: In the 1950s Drummond 'M7' 0-4-4Ts tended to monopolise the Seaton branch. On 3 August 1958 No 30046 pauses at Colyton with a train for Seaton Junction consisting of an ex-LSWR 'ironclad' set converted for push-pull operation.

Left: The abundance of standardised pre-cast concrete structures at Colyford typified the work of the SR plant at Exmouth Junction in the 1930s. On the same day as the previous photograph No 30046 is propelling its train in the direction of Seaton. Today crossing protection is still provided, but for trams instead of trains.

Below: In the 1930s the Southern rebuilt Seaton station on a generous scale to cope with the influx of through coaches detached from main-line trains at Seaton Junction and increasing numbers of visitors and excursionists as the resort grew in popularity. The station was a breezy place adjacent to the salt marshes of the Axe estuary.

Left: No 30046 and the branch train are dwarfed by the vastness of the station at Seaton on 3 August 1958. Note the single-engine locomotive shed, coal stage and water tower. The Bulleid corridor coach from Waterloo, visible on the right, was detached at Seaton Junction.

Left: The intrusion of suburban-style 1930s architecture at Seaton was incongruous and more evocative of the Chessington South line than a relatively quiet South Devon coastal branch. Today's Seaton Tramway veers away from the former rail line and the site of the old station on the edge of town before reaching a new and separate terminus. Seaton and Exmouth were the only resorts on the stretch of coast separating West Bay, Dorset, and the Exe estuary with stations adjoining the shore.

BRANCHES TO EXMOUTH

Right: The first station on the branch from Sidmouth Junction served the historic town of Ottery St Mary, which, despite its branch-line status, was linked to Waterloo by through coaches detached at Sidmouth Junction during the holiday season. Cross-country connections reached a high point with the advent of a short-lived Cleethorpes-Exmouth seasonal service from 1960 until 1962. After closure in 1967 much of the station site was redeveloped for industrial purposes while the station building, seen here on 11 July 1952, now functions as a youth club.

Right: Newton Poppleford was the quintessential East Devon branch-line station both in name and ambiance. This is a view north up the Otter Valley towards Tipton St Johns in July 1964.

Left: 'M7s' monopolised the Exeter Central-Exmouth service, and on 2 July 1952 No 30028 slows for the stop at Woodbury Road (since renamed Exton). In common with most other branch stations along the eastern bank of the Exe estuary, it survives as an unstaffed halt but with an improved service.

Below: With the passing of the 'M7' tanks branch services to Sidmouth and to Exmouth via Budleigh Salterton were taken over by BR Standard tanks. In April 1960 No 82011 hurries through the fields north of Ottery St Mary with a train from Sidmouth. *G. R. Siviour*

HEMYOCK BRANCH

Left: The Culm Valley light railway from Tiverton Junction to Hemyock was a quaint backwater whose lifeblood was bulk milk from the large dairy at the end of the line. Severe operating restrictions limited motive power to the light-footed '14xx' class 0-4-2Ts, while passengers on mixed trains travelled in vintage ex-Barry Railway coaches whose prime role was to provide braking capacity apart from accommodation for the visiting enthusiast and unhurried local passenger with time on his hands. No 1435 has no milk tankers for Hemyock on this occasion as it calls at Uffculme on 12 July 1952.

Below: Apart from brightening the day of the small boy on the platform, the arrival of the Hemyock train at Culmstock on the same day was little more than an opportunity to while away a few minutes to ensure that the train did not run ahead of schedule.

Right: After arriving at Hemyock on 12 July 1952 with its solitary passenger there was plenty of time for the crew to brew up before commencing some leisurely shunting.

Below: Having stowed away the Barry Railway coach, it is time for No 1435 to take on water before collecting several milk tanks to add to the next mixed train for Tiverton Junction. This slightly surrealistic railway surprisingly carried passengers until 1963, adopted diesel traction and finally vanished from the railway map in 1975 when the milk factory closed. A recent visit to Hemyock yielded little evidence of the existence of this obscure byway or the industry upon which it had depended.

2. 'THE WITHERED ARM'

EXETER TO PLYMOUTH VIA OKEHAMPTON

Above: How are the mighty fallen! A solitary 'bubble car', seen here at Sampford Courtenay station en route from Exeter to Okehampton in April 1971, provides the last remnant of a regular passenger service on the former LSWR Plymouth main line from Coleford Junction (Yeoford) to Okehampton, which ceased in 1972. However, as a result of the continuing need for rail access to Meldon Quarry, the line remained open for ballast trains. In 1997 Devon County Council began to subsidise a summer Sunday passenger service from Exeter to Okehampton and 2004 saw the restoration and reopening of Sampford Courtenay by the Dartmoor Railway.

Left: In happier days passengers from London usually changed trains at Okehampton for the Bude and Padstow lines where, as in this August 1955 scene, a trusty old Drummond 'Greyhound' would provide the power.
G. R. Siviour

Right: Okehampton station lost its through trains to both London and Plymouth in 1971 and the future of the remaining shuttle service from Exeter was hanging by a thread. Then the prospect of the station becoming a Mecca for enthusiasts and tourists seemed very unlikely.

Below: The 'Greyhounds' were renowned for their longevity and the 60-year-old veterans could still perform well on less demanding duties in their last stronghold in the West Country. In April 1960 one of the survivors takes the 9.56am Okehampton-Bude train across the magnificent Meldon viaduct just to the west of the quarry, where the line crosses the West Okement river, providing passengers with a fine view of Dartmoor, which can still be enjoyed by hikers and cyclists using the Granite Way. *G. R. Siviour*

Above: The Southern Railway terminus at Plymouth Friary was always relatively quiet and definitely subservient to the much busier establishment at North Road. On 3 March 1956 'N' class 2-6-0 No 31849 awaits departure with a stopping train for Exeter Central via the north Dartmoor route.

Below: On 4 March 1956 the dignified stone buildings at Plymouth Friary contrast markedly with the then war-scarred wooden structure at North Road. It was not, however, surprising to learn of the termination of all Southern services there in 1958 and the subsequent designation of Friary as a freight concentration centre. The gradual decline thereafter in freight traffic and the subsequent closure of Tavistock Junction yard resulted in the transfer of remaining freight marshalling functions to Friary in 1973.

TAW VALLEY AND ILFRACOMBE LINES

Right: Lapford was an important station on the Taw Valley line due to the large dairy products plant of Cow & Gate Foods and, after a merger, Unigate. Large quantities of milk were shipped in six-wheeled tank wagons, two of which are visible here on 26 August 1970. This was an important source of rail freight revenue until the company closed its Lapford plant and moved to Torrington in the 1970s. Within a few years all bulk milk traffic in Devon and Cornwall, which was for many years very prominent at such diverse country railheads as Seaton Junction, Hemyock and Lifton, was lost to road competition. Lapford now has only a skeletal passenger service and the Taw Valley line no longer carries freight.

Above: Portsmouth Arms, now an unstaffed halt at which only a few trains stop by request, took its name from an adjacent pub. The all too familiar signs of the basic railway characterise this view, also taken on 26 August 1970, looking towards Kings Nympton, which formerly rejoiced in the particularly optimistic name of South Molton Road (the town of South Molton was more than 10 miles distant on the GWR's Taunton-Barnstaple line).

Right: Umberleigh station, its spacious right of way evidence of its broad gauge ancestry, retains an active passing loop, at which all trains now stop. This view, taken on the same day as the previous ones, is looking in a southerly direction towards Portsmouth Arms.

Left: The penultimate station on the northern section of the truncated SR main line from Exeter to Ilfracombe is that of Chapelton, also seen on 26 August 1970. With an infrequent service, a tenuous grip on life is maintained by this former main line as a community rail partnership.

Right: In 1970 Barnstaple Junction was still the most important intermediate station on the downgraded former SR main line from Exeter to the coastal resort of Ilfracombe. However, the extensive yard was witnessing its final days, time was running out on the Ilfracombe line and the principal town of North Devon, which once boasted three stations, was shortly to endure another round of rationalisation destined to reduce the rail presence to the sadly diminished remnant that remains of the former Barnstaple Junction (now just plain 'Barnstaple') today.

Below: 'Battle of Britain' class light Pacific No 34061 *73 Squadron* leaves Barnstaple Junction with an Ilfracombe-Exeter train in April 1964. *G. R. Siviour*

Right: Decay is ravaging the former GWR station at Barnstaple Victoria Road on 26 August 1970, six months after the end of goods services on the Taunton line. During the 1960s the poorly located GWR station on the periphery of the town had experienced rapid decline with diversion of passenger services between there and Taunton to Barnstaple Junction in June 1960, followed by the withdrawal of passenger services on the former GWR route in October 1966 and finally the end of goods traffic in March 1970.

Left: The track layout at Barnstaple Junction remained deceptively impressive in the summer of 1970, despite the fact that the branch to Fremington and Torrington (on the left) had lost its passenger services five years earlier and was destined to lose its remaining freight service in 1982, while the former main line to Ilfracombe (to the right) was due for complete closure in a few months.

Left: This is the view from the same vantage point looking south on the same day. When this station became the railhead for North Devon in October 1970 the track layout was greatly modified, leaving only that serving the main platform.

Left: Barnstaple Town station, seen here on 21 July 1955, was the closest to the town centre. A short distance beyond the level crossing the line from Barnstaple Junction crossed the River Taw on a sharply curved bridge.

Below: In 1898 Barnstaple Town station had replaced an earlier structure on a nearby site known as Barnstaple Quay. Seen on the same day as the previous picture, note the former bay platform on the left, which was used by the narrow-gauge trains of the Lynton & Barnstaple Railway until the premature closure of that scenic route in 1936. The station building is now used by the local authority for educational purposes.

Right: The last days on the Ilfracombe line, which had been reduced to the lowly status of a basic railway operated by DMUs and shorn of its goods service, were typified by this 26 August 1970 scene of an Exeter train at the once popular but now deserted station of Mortehoe & Woolacombe. The chequered career of the station after closure saw its use as an unsuccessful theme park for children before becoming part of an affordable housing and holiday cottage scheme for today's car-dependent visitors.

Right: 'N' class Mogul No 31851 shunts the once busy goods yard at Mortehoe in April 1964. *G. R. Siviour*

Below: The Mortehoe-Ilfracombe section of the line was notable for its curvature, gradients and scenery. 'Battle of Britain' No 34080 *74 Squadron* approaches Mortehoe with an Exeter train, also in April 1964. *G. R. Siviour*

Below: There were few scenes as sad as those of stations serving seaside resorts that had been largely forsaken by travellers as travel habits changed and holidaymakers switched to their recently acquired cars. In its last days the spacious hilltop station overlooking the town of Ilfracombe hardly resembled the formerly busy terminus of the 'Devon Belle' and 'Atlantic Coast Express'. On 26 August 1970 the threat of imminent abandonment is palpable. The large and derelict structure on the right was the goods shed. The station was subsequently demolished and replaced by an office block.

BARNSTAPLE JUNCTION TO TORRINGTON

Above: Nestling on the southern bank of the lower tidal reaches of the River Taw, the small station of Fremington was the location where ball clay from the mines at Peters Marland and Meeth was transhipped from rail to coastal vessels. The quay was adjacent to the up platform, which was noted for its elevated signalbox, seen here on 21 July 1955. Clay exports ceased at the end of 1969 due to the physical deterioration of the dockside cranes, and the quay was closed in March 1970. Thereafter ball clay shipments followed a circuitous routeing to Fowey docks. The former railway buildings have been 're-created' to assure a new role for the site as a visitor attraction on the Tarka Trail.

Below: The oldest power normally assigned to a named train in 1955 was probably represented by the 'M7' class 0-4-4Ts. On 21 July No 30250 is seen at Fremington with the Torrington section of the 'Atlantic Coast Express'. The sidings serving the quay used by the ball clay trains are visible on the left.

Above: This is Instow station, looking east, also on 21 July 1955. Following closure in 1965 the signalbox was preserved and is now a landmark on the Tarka Trail. The station buildings are the headquarters of the local yacht club, but in the 1950s the Torrington section of the 'Atlantic Coast Express' stopped here and the goods yard was flourishing.

Below: On the same day, No 30250 is now heading a relatively heavy mixed working from Barnstaple Junction to Torrington at Instow. Note the milk tank wagons for Torrington at the rear of the train.

Left: Appropriately for the most important town on the line, Bideford was provided with more impressive station facilities, as seen here on 21 July 1955. Located adjacent to the medieval bridge across the River Torridge, the station was close to the terminus of the standard-gauge Bideford, Westward Ho! & Appledore Railway, which, however, lasted only from 1901 until 1917.

Below: Drummond 'M7' No 30250 is seen again on its 'top link duty', pausing at Bideford on the same day with the Torrington section of the 'ACE'.

Right: In August 1964, with only a few months remaining before the withdrawal of passenger services on the branch from Barnstaple Junction, there is nonetheless plenty of activity at Torrington station. No 42108 is taking water after arriving with the branch train. On the extreme left an icon of West Country bus services, a Bedford OB, providing the shuttle service to the town, waits at the station. Overlooking an inadequate North British Type 2 diesel-hydraulic waiting to depart from the up platform is a row of the ubiquitous railway cottages.

THE NORTH DEVON & CORNWALL JUNCTION LIGHT RAILWAY

Above: The quiet, rural atmosphere of Torrington station was intermittently disturbed by periods of busy rail activity. On 21 July 1955 the down platform has just been vacated by 'M7' tank No 30250, which waits in a siding to the east of the station with the branch passenger train from Barnstaple Junction, while the stock for the morning mixed train for Halwill Junction waits hopefully for patrons. This most obscure of Southern branch-line services will be hauled by veteran 'E1R' tank No 32608, the smoke of which is visible beyond the station.

Right: The writer was the only passenger travelling on the morning mixed train from Halwill Junction which has just arrived at Torrington on the same day. The thin sprinkling of passengers awaiting the next service for Barnstaple attests to the inconvenient location of the station, some two miles from the town. In the Southern Railway era Torrington was superseded by Ilfracombe as the principal North Devon railhead for passenger services, although it retained its own two-coach section of the 'Atlantic Coast Express'. After closure to passengers in 1965, and before the end of general freight traffic in 1978, Torrington experienced a short-lived expansion in bulk milk business and a brief survival of its goods shed as a fertiliser depot until 1980. The end came with the loss of the ball clay shipments from Peters Marland and Meeth in 1982. The station building remained and was reincarnated in 1984 as the 'Puffing Billy' pub, serving hikers and cyclists using the Tarka Trail, which was created on former railway rights of way between Braunton and Meeth.

Left: On 21 July 1955 'E1R' class No 32608 makes a brief photo stop with the morning mixed train from Halwill Junction at the isolated and shelterless platform of Watergate Halt. Behind the camera is the viaduct that replaced the original wooden structure of its predecessor, the 3-foot-gauge Marland Light Railway, which dated from 1880.

Below: An incongruous row of ball clay workers' cottages was situated in a rural setting adjoining Yarde Halt, where the Torrington train waits in order to maintain its camera-friendly schedule on the same day.

Left: A busy moment on a forgotten light railway: No 32608, with its Torrington-bound train, meets classmate No 32610 on a down freight on the passing loop at Petrockstow. This group of ten 0-6-2Ts were 1927-28 Maunsell rebuilds of former LB&SCR 'E1' 0-6-0Ts dating from 1874-83, which were selected for rebuilding after being rendered redundant by electrification in the London area. Equipped with an additional pony truck and large coal bunker they were well suited to light railway conditions as well as banking duties between Exeter St Davids and Exeter Central, but 1955 was to be the final year of operation for these veterans on the Torrington-Halwill line.

Above: Unlikely power for a light railway during the final era of passenger service is this North British Type 2 'D63xx' class diesel-hydraulic loco, about to leave Petrockstow with the 7.55am short working for Torrington on a misty August morning in 1964.

Below: During the same month, and with a single passenger on board, No 41216 tackles the gradient between Meeth Halt and Hatherleigh with the morning Torrington-Halwill train consisting of one Bulleid composite coach.

Left: Meeth offered the passenger slightly superior facilities compared to some of the other halts, in terms of shelter from the elements and a platform bench. The arrival of the morning Torrington train on 21 July 1955 allows a break for gossip while the fireman ponders the sanity of those who travel great distances to record such mundane but rapidly vanishing scenes such as this.

Below: Hatherleigh, with a population of little more than a thousand, was the largest intermediate community on the light railway, although its station was two miles from the sleepy town. The shortage of passengers there was partly offset by livestock, farm supplies and parcels traffic.

Right: A peaceful light railway vignette at Hatherleigh as No 32608 takes on water en route from Halwill to Torrington on 21 July 1955. The provision of an open ground frame controlling access to the passing loop and siding is typical of the very basic infrastructure on this bucolic and meandering backwater and was in the best tradition of 'light railway magnate' Colonel Stephens, who engineered the construction of the line.

Above: During August 1964 No 41216 slows to five miles per hour for one of several ungated level crossings between Hatherleigh and Hole with the morning mixed train to Halwill consisting of a Bulleid composite coach, three loaded ball clay wagons and a brake-van.

Below: The two enthusiasts travelling in the brake-van of the train represented an exceptional passenger load, as time was running out for all services beyond Hatherleigh.

Above: An assignment to Hole (for Black Torrington) was not the most demanding job for station staff and the prevailing rural tranquillity is scarcely disturbed by the arrival of No 32608 and its empty train bound for Torrington on 21 July 1955. The solitary platform lamp seems to exemplify the loneliness of the station named after nothing more significant than a local farm.

Below: The North Devon & Cornwall Junction Light Railway maintained a very low profile at Halwill, where it paralleled the Bude line for the final mile with only a backshunt connection near the station. Change was nonetheless occurring on 16 July 1955 as modern steam power such as 2-6-2T No 41295 was supplanting the 'E1Rs'. Note the incongruity in the mismatch of old and new represented by this train as it approaches the end of a leisurely run from Torrington.

Above: A short bare platform connected to the main station by footpath emphasised the lowly status of the light railway at Halwill. Following arrival and run-round No 41295 hopefully waits for a rare adventurous soul who might arrive on the next down train, while a connecting service to Okehampton and points east is ready to depart from the up platform.

Below: Motive power on the lines radiating from Halwill was never entirely predictable in the 1950s, as typified by this traditional assemblage of 'E1R' No 32608 and LSWR coach, which has just arrived from Torrington on 21 July 1955.

HALWILL TO BUDE

Above: Grimy BR Standard Class 3 2-6-2T No 82011 calls at Dunsland Cross with a Bude-Halwill local train on 21 July 1955. The remote location of this station suggests that it was not built in response to any obvious business pressure. Named for a nearby rural crossroads, it was close to Dunsland House (an historic mansion sadly destroyed by fire in 1967) and a row of railway cottages, while its name board advised passengers to alight for Shebbear College (a boarding school situated several miles away). The station retained its original single-storey building similar to those at Halwill and Ashbury & North Lew. Although it ceased to handle sand shipments from Bude Wharf in 1942, wagonload consignments of roadstone and livestock feed continued to be received until freight services were withdrawn in 1964.

Left: In April 1960 'T9' No 30715 hustles the Bude branch train through the forestry plantations west of Dunsland Cross.
G. R. Siviour

Right: For 17 years from 1879 the market town of Holsworthy was the terminus of a branch line from Halwill. With the completion of the extension to Bude, the station became a regional centre for the livestock industry and served a slaughterhouse. Seen here on 13 July 1955, the hand carts on the platform may have been relics from the days when Holsworthy was also a focal collection and distribution point for the Royal Mail. In later years the station continued to deal with farm supplies and household coal, while the rake of livestock wagons at the western end of the up platform testifies to the longevity of this erstwhile traffic, which was destined to continue for nearly ten more years.

Right: All is quiet between train times in this view looking east at Holsworthy on the same day. The station master's house and its adjoining greenhouse add an atmosphere of domesticity. Although today it is more than 40 years since the last train called, the station site is still a busy local distribution centre for the farm sector. To the west of Holsworthy sections of the former right of way, including the concrete Derriton Viaduct, have been converted to a hiking trail.

Left: In spite of its inconvenient situation some distance from the villages it purported to serve, Whitstone & Bridgerule station was a surprisingly commodious establishment, which on 13 July 1955 still boasted its original LSWR enamel name boards. The change in levels of the down platform marks the site of the temporary trailing points which give access to military sidings that were added in 1943. Not far beyond the road bridge the branch entered Cornwall for the final few miles to the terminus at Bude. The station handled a steady volume of farm supplies and coal until closure.

Above: Bude was quite an impressive terminus, and on 22 July 1955 the station staff were busy with parcels traffic and the W. H. Smith bookstall is open for business. The goods shed is visible beyond the station canopy.

Below: On the same day 'T9' 4-4-0 No 30709 has just arrived with a local from Okehampton. It will move forward to the headshunt before reversing beyond its train to the turntable at the locomotive shed, which is out of sight in the distance.

Right: Bude station was no great distance from the town centre, something of an exception for North Cornwall. Its two platforms reflected the needs of the summertime peak traffic of an earlier period and appeared somewhat generous for the short trains that were typical of the last decade of operations.

Right: The extensive station building at Bude, seen here on 18 July 1955, was of an attractive style adopted by the LSWR at the end of the 19th century and reminiscent of those on the Meon Valley line. Sadly all this apparent solidity and permanence was an illusion and the site was swallowed up by housing development after closure.

Below: On the same day Standard Class 3 2-6-2T No 82011 is shunting on the Bude canal wharf where coal, stockfeed and fertiliser traffic continued until 1960. With the opening of the railway most of the unfinished canal was abandoned. An unusual feature of this waterway was the use of wheeled tub boats that ran on inclined planes such as that at Hobbacott Down, the remains of which are visible near Whitstone & Bridgerule station.

NORTH CORNWALL LINE

Left: Stopping trains covered the 49¾ miles, with 11 intermediate stops between Halwill and Padstow, in approximately 1hr 50min. Lightweight trains were well within the capacity of the still sprightly 55-year-old 'Greyhounds', which were predominant on the North Cornwall line. On 16 July 1955 No 30709 is about to leave the deserted platforms of Halwill on the next stage of its rural ramble from Padstow to Okehampton. Halwill (for Beaworthy) was the epitome of a country junction where long periods of tranquillity were punctuated by sudden bursts of activity as trains, as distinct from people, made connections and wagons were shunted in a desultory manner in the yard.

Left: After arrival at Halwill on 21 July 1955, 'T9' 4-4-0 No 30717 has pulled forward with the Padstow portion of the train from Okehampton leaving the rear two coaches and van, which will be taken forward to Bude by a Class 4 2-6-4T.

Left: Halwill, apart from being a regional hub for passenger services, also dealt with a steady volume of freight traffic. This 16 July 1955 view east towards Ashbury & North Lew reveals a cluster of station buildings dating from the Devon & Cornwall Railway and LSWR eras, together with ugly pre-cast 'accretions' manufactured by the SR plant at Exmouth Junction. Within the yard the 50-foot turntable had seen little use since tank engines had taken over light railway duties decades earlier. However, building and farm supply merchants continued to be the mainstay of the freight business in later years in addition to a small slaughterhouse. Now this hub of activity has been transformed into an unremarkable residential development in the depths of the countryside.

Right: An 'N' class Mogul, in making a rapid getaway from Halwill with a Padstow-Okehampton train, casts a trail of smoke across the expansive landscape of the thinly populated Devon/ Cornwall border during August 1964. On the horizon the junction and its attendant village are prominent. This seemingly immutable scene was on the threshold of changes that would soon remove the sight and sound of the railway for ever.

Right: Ashwater was the first of the typically quiet country stations encountered on the North Cornwall line after leaving Halwill. Nestling in the valley of the Carey and flanked by woodland, it was an enchanting spot almost a mile distant from the village. In this view south towards Tower Hill on 13 July 1955 the yard is almost bereft of goods traffic. Surprisingly, 40 years after closure, a coal merchant was still active there and the station survived as a residence. Ashwater demonstrates the degree of relative isolation that afflicted much of the area following the Beeching rationalisation measures. The village now has a weekly bus link to each of the regional centres of Holsworthy, Bideford and Tavistock.

Below: On the same day 'N' class Mogul No 31832 hurries along with an Okehampton stopping train north of Ashwater.

Left: Also seen on 13 July 1955, Tower Hill station was opened in 1896 on the first part of the North Cornwall line between Halwill and Launceston. Platform gravel is well raked and flowers lovingly tended in this view north towards Ashwater – altogether a great contrast with its London counterpart!

Left: The solid if sober bluestone station at Tower Hill served a scattering of small hamlets and was, in common with many others on the North Cornwall line, a very, very quiet place.

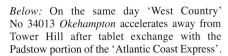

Below: On the same day 'West Country' No 34013 *Okehampton* accelerates away from Tower Hill after tablet exchange with the Padstow portion of the 'Atlantic Coast Express'.

Right: 'N' class 2-6-0 No 31836 has just crossed the bridge over the GWR line from Plymouth on the eastern edge of Launceston with a Halwill-Wadebridge goods working on 15 July 1955.

Below: Designed by Maunsell and built at Woolwich Arsenal in 1924, 'N' class No 31832 leaves Launceston for Okehampton on the same day. Beyond can be seen the spur built in 1943 connecting the GWR and SR and the line leading to the GWR station from which passenger services were diverted in 1947.

Right: Former GWR '4575' 2-6-2 No 4591 is seen on the connecting spur in the midst of a freight transfer at Launceston. Part of the former GWR yard and loco shed is visible behind the train.

Above: With its GWR neighbour, the former LSWR station at Launceston was situated on the edge of town, its architecture compatible with its surroundings. Note the quite extensive GWR goods facilities to the left in this 13 July 1955 view. Today the acreage once occupied by the railway at Launceston has been obliterated by an industrial estate, although the terminus of a narrow-gauge steam line now occupies the former North Cornwall line near the old SR station site.

Left: '4575' 2-6-2T No 4590 has just arrived at the SR station with a train from Plymouth on the scenic route via Tavistock South and Lydford. This was the first line to reach Launceston and closed in 1962.

Above: On 15 July 1955 No 31832 pauses at Launceston with an Okehampton train comprising a blend of Bulleid and Maunsell passenger stock. Regrettably the provision of such generous accommodation appeared to be excessive even during the height of the summer season.

Below: The former LSWR station at Launceston slumbers in the summer July sunshine. Beyond the bridge the line resumed its meandering westerly course towards Padstow.

Above: Egloskerry station is seen on 15 July 1955, looking east towards Launceston. Note that the platforms are lit exclusively by oil lamps. After closure in 1966 this station, like many others along the line, became a private residence.

Below: This was the view looking west towards Tresmeer. Each station on the North Cornwall line possessed a passing loop and a regularly staffed signalbox, features that doubtless inflated the operating expenses incurred by the line.

Above: On 15 July 1955 another of the redoubtable 'Greyhounds', No 30711, follows the winding course of the Kensey Valley west of Egloskerry with an Okehampton train, as its throaty exhaust, mellifluous clank of coupling rods and regular beat of carriage wheels on jointed track echo around the hills. Such commonplace sounds are now a rapidly fading memory except on preserved heritage lines.

Right: 'West Country' No 34004 *Yeovil* stops at the empty platform at Tresmeer with an all-stations train for Padstow on the same day. Tresmeer station was actually closer to the hamlet of Splatt, but perhaps the LSWR deemed that an inappropriate name for a station.

Right: Following the train's departure around the curve towards Otterham the well-manicured station at Tresmeer, almost a clone of Egloskerry, slumbers on. Today the station is an equally well maintained private residence.

Left: During August 1964 the up 'Atlantic Coast Express', in the capable hands of 'Battle of Britain' class light Pacific No 34065 *Hurricane*, arrives at Tresmeer. The provision of a four-coach Padstow section was unusual except on Saturdays.

Below: A solid stone bridge framed the route from Tresmeer to Egloskerry and the east, epitomising the long-term commitment of the LSWR to serving the district when the line was built between 1886 and 1899.

Bottom: On 20 July 1955 'T9' 4-4-0 No 30709 makes an early morning stop at Otterham en route to Okehampton with a typical lightweight train consisting of two Bulleid coaches and two vans.

Right: This view of Otterham station, looking towards Tresmeer on the same day, reflects its lonely location some two miles from the village. The 'Atlantic Coast Express' stopped at Otterham as it was a railhead for Boscastle and other coastal attractions.

Below: An empty train passes through an empty pastoral landscape east of Otterham in April 1960: 'Greyhound' No 30715 drifts downhill heading for Okehampton with a train from Padstow. *G. R. Siviour*

Left: Camelford station was more than a mile from the ancient town, and is now the British Cycling Museum. In more prosperous times bus connections for coastal resorts would await travellers in the station approach road.

Left: Apart from the platform canopy, which suggested its greater importance, Camelford was similar in its atmosphere of remoteness to most other stations on the North Cornwall line. This view is dated 19 July 1955.

Above: Goods trains were not a common feature on the North Cornwall line although the large slate quarry at Delabole generated a significant amount of traffic. On 19 July 1955 'N' class 2-6-0 No 31848 is shunting the quarry sidings with a train that includes cattle wagons catering for traffic that had been traditionally important in the district.

Right: Villagers await the arrival of visitors on the down 'Atlantic Coast Express' at the rather bleak Delabole station. Beyond the down platform wisps of steam are emanating from No 31848 as it shunts the quarry sidings.

Right: The much reduced Padstow section of the 'Atlantic Coast Express', with No 34013 *Okehampton* at the head, duly arrives and makes its daily stop at Delabole. The slate quarry sidings are visible to the right, with No 31848 shunting east of the station.

Left: The open, windswept and rolling landscape of North Cornwall defied the efforts of railway builders to reach the attractive coastal villages along the rocky wave-lashed Atlantic shore. Undeterred, the LSWR optimistically christened this station Port Isaac Road, although it was more than three miles distant from the famous fishing village and resort. It was photographed on 19 July 1955.

Below: 'T9' 4-4-0 No 30718 is very much at home on a short Padstow-Okehampton train as it tackles the curves through hilly country to the west of Port Isaac Road in April 1960.
G. R. Siviour

Above: St Kew Highway, although some distance from the older village of St Kew, was so named because of its position on what is now the A39 trunk road. This isolated station, also seen on 19 July 1955, was the last before the line followed the Camel estuary to Wadebridge and the coast.

Right: In April 1960 Class 2 2-6-2T No 41275 accelerates away from Wadebridge with a Bodmin North train along the banks of the River Camel where the North Cornwall and Bodmin lines pursued parallel but separate alignments. The cluster of buildings in the background include the station and town of Wadebridge. *G. R. Siviour*

Right: In the 1950s Wadebridge attracted much attention as the home of the three surviving '0298' class 2-4-0T Beattie well tanks, which had been retained for working the Wenford Bridge branch. Another duty allocated to them was that of station pilot, which on 19 July 1955 is being performed by No 30586. These wonderful relics also handled occasional local passenger workings between Wadebridge and Padstow. The trio were replaced by '1366' class pannier tanks in 1962 although their antiquity and uniqueness saved two from the scrapyard.

Right: No 30711 awaits the green flag at the harbourside terminus at Padstow with a stopping train for Okehampton in July 1955. This outpost of the Southern is now better known for its gustatory delights than its long-lost railway. *G. R. Siviour*

Below: The traveller from Wadebridge to Bodmin had the choice of two routes. Those with a GWR preference could opt for the service to Bodmin General (always a somewhat puzzling nomenclature) and onwards to Bodmin Road on the Paddington-Penzance main line. On 19 July 1955 '45xx' 2-6-2T No 4508 has arrived with a short train from Bodmin General. Note the loco shed and water tower to the right of the train.

Right: The Southern route from Wadebridge to Bodmin deposited the traveller at the inconveniently placed North station, but it was a journey that enabled one to retrace the route of Cornwall's pioneer Bodmin & Wadebridge Railway. In the 1950s this service was the domain of the redoubtable Adams 'O2' class 0-4-4T locomotives; on 19 July 1955 one of them, No 30200, pauses at Wadebridge with a Bodmin North-Padstow train. In the 1950s the halts between Wadebridge and Bodmin were served only by the Southern service. Railways are now only a distant memory at Wadebridge, although some vestiges remain in and around the John Betjeman Centre at the station site. The poet would doubtless approve.

3. SOUTH DEVON BRANCHES

TEIGN VALLEY BRANCH

Left: Peace and quiet no longer reign at the site of Chudleigh station where a section of the old Teign Valley line from near Heathfield to the edge of Chudleigh village has disappeared under the A38 trunk road, thereby negating the possibility of the old railway being revived as a possible alternative to the increasingly vulnerable coastal route of the main line at Dawlish and Teignmouth. This photograph was taken in June 1958. *G. R. Siviour*

Below: A trip on the Teign Valley line, which pursued a circuitous route through outstandingly beautiful Devon countryside, provided a most pleasurable alternative, for the connoisseur of railway backwaters, to the undoubted maritime delights of the main line between Exeter and Newton Abbot. Milk churns are much in evidence at Trusham in June 1958, as the signalman hands over the staff. *G. R. Siviour*

Above: A classic GWR solution to light-density branch-line operating costs, an auto-train leaves Trusham and continues its wanderings through idyllic countryside on its way to Exeter St Davids in June 1958. *G. R. Siviour*

Below: The sleepy country station of Christow was busier when the local quarries were thriving, but peace had returned by 1958 when '57xx' 0-6-0PT No 3677 departed with its solitary coach for Exeter St Davids. *G. R. Siviour*

MORETONHAMPSTEAD BRANCH

Left: Moretonhampstead, a small market town on the edge of Dartmoor, was the terminus of a delightful branch line from Newton Abbot. On 9 July 1952 '14xx' class 0-4-2T No 1427 has just arrived at the fine train shed of the old Moretonhampstead & South Devon Railway. Although passenger trains ceased in 1959, freight services lingered on until 1964. In recognition of the tourism potential of the area the GWR opened the Manor House Hotel just outside the town in 1929; it passed to the British Transport Commission following rail nationalisation, and still functions, albeit under a different name and ownership. The final removal of track north of Bovey occurred in 1966, 100 years after the opening of the original broad gauge line. The station site is still discernible although partly obscured by a road haulage depot.

Below: Six years later, in June 1958, No 1427 was still working on the Moretonhampstead branch and is taking water at the terminus. Note the attractive single-engine locomotive shed on the right. *G. R. Siviour*

ASHBURTON BRANCH

Right: The north end of the Totnes to Ashburton branch suffered the double indignity of abandonment followed by conversion to a trunk highway. One of the ubiquitous '14xx' class 0-4-2Ts, No 1439, is in the process of shunting its auto-trailer at the delightful terminus at Ashburton in June 1955. Fate was kinder to the Totnes-Buckfastleigh section of the line, which continues to prosper as the South Devon Railway, one of Devon's foremost heritage lines, where steam is king. *G. R. Siviour*

Right: Buckfastleigh station has now been transformed from a quiet intermediate stop on the somnolent Totnes-Ashburton branch line into a popular Mecca for enthusiasts and tourists. At a quieter time No 1439 is the power for the branch train. *G. R. Siviour*

Below: No 1439 leaves Totnes main-line station with a train for Ashburton in June 1955. South Devon Railway services now use a new station at Littlehempston, which is accessible by footpath from the national network station. *G. R. Siviour*

KINGSWEAR/DARTMOUTH

Above: The GWR station at Dartmouth was unique as its passenger service was provided exclusively by ferry from the nearby railhead at Kingswear. In the days before the motor van the freight connection was provided by waterborne horse and cart. *Author's collection*

KINGSBRIDGE BRANCH

Below: It is hard to believe that the one-time archetypal country junction of Brent has vanished, leaving only a double-track main line along which HSTs and 'Voyagers' now race past. Gone are the generations of holidaymakers bound for summer relaxation in the South Hams who changed here and took the branch train to Kingsbridge. In April 1960 typical power is being provided by '45xx' 2-6-2T No 4561, which is awaiting the arrival of a down main-line service. *G. R. Siviour*

Right: Occupying the midpoint of the line was the bucolic station of Gara Bridge, where trains could cross at a cleft in the hills shared with the River Avon. In April 1960 No 4561 makes a characteristically purposeful GW getaway with the branch train returning to Brent. *G. R. Siviour*

Left: No 4561 looks very much at home amidst the pastoral landscape of the South Hams near Gara Bridge as it heads for Kingsbridge.
G. R. Siviour

Right: The terminus at the little town of Kingsbridge, in common with nearby Kingswear, offered travellers the option of continuing their journey by ferry, in this case to the charming resort of Salcombe. Preference for the family car resulted in the Kingsbridge branch withering on the vine and finally succumbing in 1963 after inevitable downgrading of infrastructure and dieselisation. The single-engine loco shed is hidden by No 4561 while the curved carriage shed could intrigue the aspiring modeller. The lengthy platforms were poignant reminders of another age in which the railway monopolised holiday travel. *G. R. Siviour*

PLYMOUTH TO LAUNCESTON

Above: The former GWR station at Tavistock South, in spite of its location on a scenic secondary route linking Plymouth with Launceston, was a more impressive establishment than that of its SR competitor on the other side of town. The trains to Plymouth were quite well patronised compared to the infrequent service to the north, which roughly paralleled the SR route to Lydford before turning west to cross the Cornwall border near Launceston. On 16 July 1955 the crew of '14xx' 0-4-2T No 1424 enjoy a tea break in the shade of the train shed before returning to the south. Ironically, the last passenger train left Tavistock South on the day before the appointment of Dr Beeching as Chairman of British Railways. After closure this historic station was destroyed and replaced by a medical centre.

Left: The GWR station at Launceston, seen here on 15 July 1955, was adjacent to but quite separate from its LSWR counterpart. Although passenger trains were diverted to the SR station as an economy measure in 1947, the former GWR yard remained very active for goods traffic.

Above: In this view from the stop blocks on the same day, the old GWR station at Launceston was in remarkably good condition eight years after the departure of the last passenger train.

Right: The railway history of Plymouth is quite complex. Among the stations that have vanished was the formidable stone terminus at Millbay, which was once the destination of boat trains connecting with ocean liners. Damaged during the Second World War, which left such serious scars on the city, it closed to passengers on 23 April 1941. Its subsequent decline was marked by a continuance of goods services until 20 June 1966, although its four platforms were used to create additional sidings for stabling rolling stock until 6 October 1969. The connecting line to North Road station was closed 30 June 1971, after which the site was redeveloped and is now the Plymouth Pavilions Leisure Complex. It is seen here on 4 March 1956.

PRINCETOWN BRANCH

Above: An overgrown ruin after closure and now a private nature reserve, the junction station at Yelverton was once popular with Plymouth commuters. On 3 March 1956 the down platform is occupied by '14xx' class 0-4-2T No 1408 with an auto-trailer on a Plymouth-Tavistock South service while '45xx' 2-6-2T No 4568 is about to take water at the curving Princetown branch platform on the left. The ominous sky is strangely appropriate, for this was the last day of train services to the GWR outpost high up on Dartmoor.

Left: A few months earlier, on 16 July 1955, '45xx' class 2-6-2T No 4524 waits in the branch platform at Yelverton for the connecting train from Plymouth before leaving for Princetown.

Above: Dousland was the only intermediate staffed station and block post on the branch, and the goods facilities and loop east of the station boasted the most impressive array of signals on this steeply graded line. Note also the sharp curvature that necessitated the provision of check rails.

Below: Beyond the yard and passing loop at Dousland loomed the brooding granite mass of Dartmoor – the challenge confronting trains destined for Princetown is obvious. These views were taken on the last day of operations, 3 March 1956.

Top: Burrator for Sheepstor Halt occupied a commanding position overlooking the dam and reservoir that is a source of the Plymouth water supply.

Above: No 4524 pauses at Burrator Halt with a Yelverton train on a fine summer's day, 16 July 1955. The scenic beauty of the Burrator reservoir was an undoubted visitor attraction.

Left: On the final day No 4568 is working hard on greasy rail at Burrator Halt as it struggles to lift a well-filled train of railway enthusiasts and nostalgic locals making a farewell trip to Princetown.

Right: No 4568 coasts downhill across the moor between Ingra Tor and Burrator halts with a return Princetown to Yelverton train on the last day. The sturdy lineside fencing protected the line from unwanted incursions by the wild Dartmoor ponies.

Right: The lonely halt at Ingra Tor was not an inviting place when the mists crept over the moor, and was renowned for its unusual notice warning hikers of the danger of snakes. Beyond the halt the line continues its tortuous climb to Princetown.

Below: Mist enshrouds the granite-strewn slopes of King Tor on 3 March 1956 as No 4568 approaches with a Yelverton train. King Tor, like other halts on the line, was accessible only on foot (or horseback). Each made excellent starting points for those intent on savouring the wilderness experience offered by Dartmoor. However, only the more experienced and hardy would venture out in conditions like this when the combination of sudden dense mists and potentially dangerous mires could threaten the unwary hiker.

Above: The terminus at Princetown was, at over 1,400ft above sea level, the highest station on the GWR. The extremes of weather, ranging from summer sunshine to the mists and snowdrifts of winter, bestowed a special character on this 'wild west' branch line. The extra protection from the moorland winds provided for passengers using the station – which was patrolled during this July 1952 visit by a particularly aggressive goat – can be seen.

Below: '45xx' 2-6-2T No 4524 has run around its train at Princetown prior to the less demanding – from the fireman's perspective – downhill run to Yelverton on 16 July 1955. Characteristically, the yard at the terminus was not a busy place in the final years.

4. CORNISH BRANCHES

LOOE BRANCH

Above: Cornwall abounded in scenic former GWR branches and one that has survived, albeit in a somewhat shrunken form, connects the main line at Liskeard with the popular coastal village of Looe. For most of its length the line follows the tranquil valley of the East Looe River but the hilly topography at the north end imposed significant impediments in terms of heavy gradients and curvature together with a reversal at Coombe Junction. In April 1960 '4575' 2-6-2T No 5557 supplies the required extra muscle near Coombe. *G. R. Siviour*

Right: '4575' 2-6-2T No 4585 has arrived at the separate Looe branch platform at Liskeard. Situated at a right angle to the main line, the branch train left in quite the wrong direction for Looe, but difficult topography imposed such contortions. The Looe branch continues to soldier on despite the oddities of its stations at Liskeard and Coombe Junction. *G. R. Siviour*

BODMIN AND WENFORD BRIDGE

Above: In the 1960s locomotives of the former GWR began to appear at Bodmin North. In April 1960 '57xx' 0-6-0PT No 4694 approaches Nanstallon Halt with a Bodmin train. The route from Bodmin North to Padstow was converted after closure in 1967 to become the Camel Trail beloved by hikers and cyclists. *G. R. Siviour*

Below: Dunmere Junction was the point where the SR line to Bodmin North swung away to the east while the gated Wenford Bridge branch began its picturesque climb to the north, as seen in this 19 July 1955 view. Both were built by the pioneer Bodmin & Wadebridge Railway in 1834.

Right: A short distance from Dunmere Junction it was necessary to protect the Wenford goods at an ungated level crossing on the A389 road from Bodmin to Wadebridge, where No 30587 awaits a green flag on 19 July 1955.

Below: Such was the climb up to Wenford Bridge that it was essential to replenish the water supply for the Beattie locomotives at the Penhargard water tank set amidst the sylvan beauty of Pencarrow Wood.

Left: There were few more delightful places on the railways of Cornwall than Pencarrow Wood. In this charming scene, photographed on 19 July 1955, No 30587 contemplates the forested route ahead as it takes water. Note the original Bodmin & Wadebridge milepost. Mineral trains had been passing this way since 1834.

Right: What looks like the archetypal English country lane is in fact the route of the Wenford Bridge branch in Pencarrow Wood! The writer has been unable to discover any records of sparks from locomotives causing conflagrations here despite the overarching forest cover.

Left: No 30587 is working hard as it rounds the Tresarrett curve on the final mile to Wenford Bridge on the same day.

Above: On 19 July 1955 No 30587 has just arrived at the Wenford china clay works, which were operated for many years by English Clay Lovering Pochin & Co Ltd. The drying sheds are visible to the left.

Below: The 5-ton-capacity overhead hoist at Wenford Bridge marked the extremity of the line in 1955, apart from the abandoned private tramway and incline to the De Lank quarries. The Southern Railway enthusiast could derive some satisfaction from the fact that to reach Wenford Bridge was to attain the most remote point on the former SR network from Waterloo.

FOWEY BRANCH

Above: Hugging the west bank of the Fowey River, the short branch from Lostwithiel to Fowey lost its passenger service in 1965. In April 1960 '14xx' No 1419 propels its train towards the junction as it nears Golant Halt. The branch has been retained for china clay traffic although Lostwithiel, on the main line, has been demoted to the status of an unstaffed station. *G. R. Siviour*

Left: In August 1955 Class '45xx' 2-6-2T No 4552 passes Fowey station with another trainload of china clay destined for the shiploading facilities nearby, while a '14xx' class 0-4-2T simmers in the bay platform with the Lostwithiel auto-train. *G. R. Siviour*